From Hurt to Healing: Transforming Painful Memories into Growth

From Hurt to Healing: Transforming Painful Memories into Growth

TABLE OF CONTENT

CHAPTER 4: CULTIVATING SELF-COMPASSION AND SELF-FORGIVENESS

CHAPTER 5: LEARNING TO LET GO THROUGH MINDFULNESS

CHAPTER 6: REWRITING YOUR NARRATIVE AND REFRAMING THE PAST

Introduction: From Pain to Possibility

Pain is an unavoidable part of the human existence. Over the course of our lives, we all encounter difficulties, face adversities, and get hurt by others or by life circumstances. These hurts can leave us feeling broken, stuck, and defined by our past. Unhealed wounds and negative experiences often lead to harmful thought patterns and destructive behaviors that hold us back from living fully and reaching our potential.

However, while pain is unavoidable, remaining trapped by our hurts is not. Within each of us exists an incredible capacity for resilience, growth, and healing. With courage, intention, and the right tools, we can break free from past hurts to create lives of purpose, joy, and connection. The journey from emotional wounds to wholeness begins when we make the choice to not just survive our past, but to learn, expand, and flourish because of it.

This book provides a roadmap for that journey. Drawing on the latest research in psychology, neuroscience, and trauma healing, as well as evidence-based therapies like Cognitive Behavioral Therapy (CBT), Eye Movement Desensitization and Reprocessing (EMDR), and mind-body practices, it guides readers step-by-step through practices for understanding, processing, and releasing chronic emotional pain in order to reclaim their lives.

The Promise of Post-Traumatic Growth

At the heart of our journey is the transformative potential of post-traumatic growth - the notion that adversity can catalyze profound positive change. While painful at the time, our lowest moments plant the seeds for increased strength, insight, appreciation for life, improved relationships, and a deeper sense of meaning. By shifting our perception, we can reframe past traumas as catalysts for a better future.

While trauma inevitably also leaves scars, the size and shape of those scars are not fixed - they are only as big as the walls we continue to build around our still-open wounds. True healing requires dismantling our defenses, becoming vulnerable, and applying the salve of self-love and self-compassion. When we approach past hurts with radically gentle acceptance rather than resistance, we deprive pain of its power over us.

Make no mistake - healing is difficult work. It asks us to challenge narratives we have long clung to, dismantle our own mental, emotional and behavioral coping strategies, and face head-on emotions we have tried desperately to avoid. But I guarantee you the effort is worthwhile. On the other side lies freedom.

Who This Book Is For

This book is for anyone seeking to break free from old wounds, destructive behavioral patterns or suffocating mental loops rooted in the past. It is for those who feel weighed down by memories, defined by trauma, or stuck replaying hurtful experiences over and over. You may have tried to "just get over it" only to have the pain resurface again and again. This book will show you how to get to the roots of hurt, process experiences in a new light, rewrite limiting narratives, and integrate lessons learned to finally be at peace in the present.

In particular, this book is for those who:

- Struggle with chronic negative thinking and critical self-talk
- Have trouble trusting others and building healthy relationships
- Engage in self-harm behaviors to cope with emotional distress
- Feel depressed, anxious, angry, cynical or detached due to past experiences
- Have low self-worth, feelings of shame, or lack sense of purpose
- Find unhealthy ways to numb or avoid painful memories and feelings
- Feel their personality or life choices were irrevocably shaped by trauma

While professional support is also highly recommended for deep-seated trauma, the tools and guidance in this book provide a starting point to begin reclaiming your freedom and catalyzing positive change.

How This Book Can Help

This book will empower you to:

- Understand how emotional wounds impact your mental, physical, and spiritual health
- Identify core painful memories and make sense of their lingering effects
- Rewrite disempowering narratives about yourself and your past
- Practice mindfulness to facilitate present moment awareness
- Develop tools to disarm negative thought patterns at their roots
- Cultivate radical self-compassion to foster acceptance and healing
- Facilitate the emotional processing of stuck grief, anger, shame, and hurt
- Recognize past pain as an opportunity for growth and meaning making
- Deprive traumatic memories of their emotional power over you

- Establish healthy boundaries and behaviors to protect your peace
- Continually grow through self-reflection, courage and resilience
- Ultimately letting go and moving forward unburdened and free

While the journey won't always be easy, it will equip you with practices and perspectives to transform your relationship with your past, reauthor your life story, and step fully into each moment with intention, wisdom, and joy.

How This Book Is Structured

The book is organized into three parts:

Part I - Understanding Your Hurts explains the impacts of emotional wounds, identifies where core hurts originate, and examines how negative experiences shape our psychology and behaviors.

Part II - Practices for Healing explores strategies and tools for processing trauma, rewriting narratives, facilitating grief, cultivating self-love and ultimately releasing the past's hold.

Part III - Moving Forward in Freedom focuses on cementing change by establishing healthy habits and making meaning to continually grow through - not just beyond - past hurts.

While designed to build upon one another, feel free to skip around to the chapters most relevant to your situation. Each chapter includes self-assessments, step-by-step exercises, mindfulness practices, journaling prompts and more to make the concepts interactive and directly applicable.

At the end of the journey, you will have gained deeper self-awareness, nurtured self-compassion, established healthy coping strategies, and be able to look back with acceptance rather than anger - no longer defining yourself by the hurts of yesterday, but looking forward with hope to all the beauty, joy and purpose tomorrow holds.

The pain of the past cannot be changed - but you can radically change how you relate to it. Let this book be your guide to shifting from hurt to healing, and embarking on the journey of a lifetime - your own.

Chapter 1: The Impact of Unhealed Wounds

Life leaves its scars on all of us. The wounds of past traumas, big and small, can linger long after the events that caused them. Like shards of glass, they pierce our sense of safety, trust, and self-worth. Yet we often minimize our own pain - believing time alone will heal, that we just need to "get over it," or that by sheer will we can banish bad memories from our minds.

But hurt ignored is not healed. Suppressed emotions inevitably resurface, triggered by present experiences that echo past pains. Unexamined wounds exert their insidious influence unconsciously, undermining our health, relationships, and purpose. In order to move forward freely into each new moment, we must proactively clean out old wounds by looking courageously inward.

This chapter explores the ways emotional injuries - from small slights to major traumas - continue shaping our psyches and behaviors long after they occur. By illuminating these impacts, we gain motivation to finally deal with pain that we've minimized or sought to bury. Healing begins when we shine a light of compassionate awareness on our darkest places.

The Brain's Response to Emotional Wounds

To understand how past hurts continue influencing our current thinking and actions requires first examining how the brain processes painful events. fMRI scans reveal that emotional trauma deeply affects our limbic system, the part of the brain governing instinctual responses, mood, motivation, and memory formation. In essence, trauma alters the very wiring of our brain.

Specifically, painful experiences activate the amygdala, the part of the limbic system that generates emotional perceptions and reactions to threats. This kicks us into "fight or flight" mode, flooding the body with cortisol and adrenaline. While vital for responding to immediate danger, chronically-activated stress responses wreak havoc on our health over time.

Simultaneously, trauma impacts the hippocampus, the center of learning and memory formation that categorizes experiences into context-based narratives. The hippocampus records traumatic events vividly because the amygdala essentially tells it, *"This is important - remember every last detail!"*

These memories get seared deeply into neural pathways as we relive the events over and over. The prefrontal cortex, which governs executive functioning, becomes impaired - making it difficult to regulate emotions or put feelings into a meaningful perspective.

In essence, unprocessed trauma generates a defective fight-or-flight response that continues overreacting to non-life-threatening stimuli, while the emotional brain keeps retrieving vivid memories of threat and pain as if they're still current. Healing involves rewiring these neurological responses.

Common Impacts of Unresolved Hurt

The downstream impacts of leaving emotional wounds untreated are far-reaching. While we all respond uniquely based on our own experiences, temperament and psychological makeup, common effects include:

1. Negative Self-Narratives: Our perception of experiences shape the narratives we construct about ourselves and the world. Trauma often generates limiting beliefs like, "I'm worthless, unlovable, or defective," "The world is dangerous," or, "People always abandon me." Over time we automatically filter new experiences through these disempowering lenses. Healing requires becoming aware of and rewriting self-limiting internal stories.

2. Diminished Self-Worth: Because our sense of identity and value stems from the accumulation of experiences, unhealed emotional wounds foster an eroded sense of self-worth. Trauma teaches us we are fundamentally unsafe and unvalued, infecting us with chronic feelings of shame, guilt, or deficiency. By cultivating self-love through compassionate practices, we can recenter our worth irrespective of the past.

3. Disconnection from Emotions: Unresolved trauma short-circuits our capacity to be present with difficult emotions. When painful feelings seem too overwhelming to bear, we detach by numbing out, ignoring anger, or suppressing grief altogether. But avoidance only amplifies pain. Healing requires cultivating mindfulness to remain present with sensations, separating emotions from our sense of identity, and learning to self-soothe difficult feelings as they arise.

4. Lack of Trust: When emotional needs are chronically unmet as children, we internalize a sense of unworthiness and develop insecure attachment styles that persist into adulthood. Painful betrayals experienced later in life also rupture our ability to trust others or be vulnerable in relationships. By rebuilding safe connections first with ourselves, then slowly with others, we counteract this emotional wariness.

5. Perfectionism: Perfectionism often develops as an attempt to regain a sense of control and worth after trauma. By holding ourselves to unrealistic standards, we try mitigating the anxiety that we are inherently defective. But this hamster wheel of shame, over-achieving, and burnout is unsustainable. We must reframe self-worth as unconditional to develop genuine self-acceptance.

6. Reactivity and Dysregulation: Unhealed pain fosters hair-trigger reactivity, where even minor stressors produce frequent emotional outbursts, anxiety attacks, or self-sabotaging choices as our brains reactively misinterpret current circumstances as past threats. Building distress tolerance through mindfulness, exercise, social support, and healthy outlets for emotions can help regulate these reactive impulses.

7. Self-Harming Behaviors: Secretly, many turn to self-harming habits like addiction, self-isolation, or self-criticism to distract from suppressed emotional wounds. Yet because these behaviors produce shame, a vicious cycle results. Developing healthy coping mechanisms to discharge emotional pain directly rather than mask it provides more sustainable relief.

8. Somatic Problems: Emotional trauma manifests physically through chronic inflammation, increased infections, heart problems, digestive issues, and autoimmune disorders. Releasing past hurts therefore improves long-term health outcomes. Integrative therapies like, meditation and acupuncture can help harmonize and restore mind-body balance.

9. A Diminished Life: Unresolved pain arrests development and narrows possibilities. We abandon dreams, interests, and loving relationships because our traumatized ego-self remains focused on seeking illusory control through perfectionism, avoidance, or self-punishment. Healing invites us to expand into life's fullness with courage and trust.

The impacts intensify the longer pain goes unprocessed. But even longstanding wounds can be healed through courage and compassion.

Common Questions About Unresolved Hurt

In my experience, several concerns commonly arise when first examining unhealed emotional wounds:

"I had traumatic experiences, but I turned out fine."
We often cling to this narrative because facing the depth of our wounds feels overwhelming. The reality is that everyone carries pain that manifests in subtle ways. Healing those hidden hurts, even from events long past, allows us to expand into greater peace and purpose.

"I wish to avoid reopening past emotional injuries by revisiting old scars."
This concern is understandable - we all want to avoid more pain. But embracing the paradox of healing is that we must gently tend to our hurting parts in order to transmute them. Ignoring wounds doesn't erase them. With courage and the right tools, we can mend old injuries to live more fully.

"I've already addressed this concern during my therapy sessions."

Therapy provides critical support, but ensures inner work continues even after it ends. Healing is a journey. By committing to daily practices and continually reframing our relationship to pain, old wounds lose their hold to free us.

"Is it selfish to give such significant attention to my personal trauma?"
On the contrary - doing your own deep inner work enables you to then hold space for others' suffering with greater compassion. Your healing benefits the world. Treat yourself kindly as you go through the journey.

"I fear that this will evoke too much distressing sentiment."
Feelings will arise; this is part of healing. But you are in the driver's seat to move through them at your own pace, grounded in practices of mindfulness, self-care and self-love. You will not be overwhelmed. Trust the process.

Putting Awareness into Action

While simply reading about trauma's impacts is informative, truly healing our emotional wounds requires ongoing introspection, embodiment practices, and brave vulnerability. This first step of building mindful awareness already begins loosening trauma's grip. We realize that beneath our habitual thoughts and behaviors exist powerful parts of ourselves waiting to be healed through compassion.

The subsequent chapters provide tangible tools to begin tending unresolved hurts, rewriting limiting narratives, constructing new healthy habits, and ultimately moving forward unburdened into each moment. While shadowy pains from the past may never disappear completely, we can emerge wiser, kinder, and more at peace for having finally embraced all aspects of ourselves with understanding and care. Our wounds become ladders we can use to ascend to greater purpose and joy.

But for now, simply getting curious about the connections between your past experiences, current thought patterns, emotional reactions, and behaviors primes your psyche for doing the deeper healing work ahead. Self-awareness alone is a profound act of self-love.

I encourage you to start a journal to explore the following reflection questions over the coming days and weeks:

- What past emotional wounds or traumas, big or small, do I minimize or avoid thinking about?

- How might those experiences still affect my current thoughts, moods and behaviors?

- What self-narratives or core beliefs might have originally developed as a protection or coping mechanism?

- How do those inner stories limit or disempower me currently?

- What aspects of my personality or perfectionistic habits could stem from past pain or insecurity?

- What self-defeating behaviors might actually be attempts to distract from suppressed hurt?

- How does emotional pain manifest in my body? What tension, aches or health issues result?

- What emotions do I chronically detach from or avoid feeling fully?

- How could I hold these hurts with more compassion rather than judgment?

- What shifts in perspective or behavior might result from honestly addressing past wounds?

Use this reflective journaling to untangle the ways past experiences unconsciously influence your self-concept, relationships, and choices today. Simply cultivating compassionate awareness of your pain is the seed out of which healing will organically arise.

Chapter 2: Identifying Core Painful Memories

In the previous chapter, we explored how unresolved emotional wounds shape our current psychology and behaviors in subtle ways. Healing begins by bringing awareness to these lingering impacts. The next step is pinpointing the specific experiences generating this chronic pain.

Just as clearing out a physical wound involves first locating the thorn or splinter at its root, identifying core memories causing lasting hurt enables us to remove their sting. While time naturally dulls acute pain into an ache, directly addressing those formative experiences allows us to rewrite their meaning and permanently release their hold on our lives.

This chapter provides guidance on how to identify particularly impactful memories deserving focused healing work. By proactively seeking out the roots of our hurt, we regain agency and control over pain that has long festered unconsciously. Our journey now transitions from observing general wounds to pinpointing specific sources ready for deeper processing.

Why Focus on Specific Memories?

You may be wondering - if emotional wounds shape us in diffuse ways, why focus on isolating certain memories over others? There are three key reasons:

1. **Specificity breeds clarity.** Vague hurt makes it hard to heal. By identifying defined moments that generated core narratives or beliefs about ourselves, we can consciously target the stories born of those experiences for revision.

2. **Details facilitate processing**. Emotional processing requires immerging into sensory and kinetic details often glossed over in our high-level memoirs. Revisiting specifics makes integration more effective.

3. **Concentrated wounds have outsized impact**. Some singular events shape our life narratives and self-concept disproportionately. Lifting the burden of those intense memories brings tangible relief. In short, isolating formative memories allows for focused processing that can permanently shift their deeply embedded neural patterning. The goal is to transform our relationship to selective memories from which generative pain sprang.

How to Identify Impactful Memories

Pinpointing specific episodes to work through requires tuning inward. Consider the following to uncover formative memories:

1. Examine repeated negative thought patterns.

Notice cognitive and self-critical loops you get stuck in. What core beliefs seem to fuel those repetitive thoughts? What past experiences might have seeded those deep beliefs?

For example, if you think things like, "I'm such a failure" or "I always mess up," this suggests a wound around perfectionism and shame. Reflect on early childhood moments of embarrassment, severe criticism/punishment, feeling different or excluded that may have catalyzed this patterning.

2. Pay attention to physical tension or pain.

The body remembers what the mind tries to forget. Notice where you habitually carry physical tightness or discomfort. What past emotional injuries might these sensory memories echo?
For instance, jaw or neck pain can reflect suppressed words or anger, back tension can indicate carrying a heavy load, and stomach issues can result from "emotional indigestion." Gently inquire what your body is trying to reveal through its metaphors.

3. Note emotional reactions or triggers.

When particular emotions arise strongly or seem out of proportion, look for connections to formative memories. If you feel suddenly furious when ignored, ashamed when criticized, or untrusting when vulnerable, explore what early experiences wired this reactive programming.

4. Consider attachment and intimacy issues.

Childhood emotional neglect, loss of caregivers, or betrayals often generate lasting insecure attachment styles. Reflect on wounds around trust, communication, self-isolation or needing control that arose in response. Pinpoint moments and relationships that seemed to plant those seeds.

5. Identify self-defeating behaviors.
Habits like self-medication, workaholism, self-harm, raging, or avoiding intimacy rarely arise randomly in a vacuum. What core hurts might your coping mechanisms aim to numb or distract from? This points to under-addressed memories needing compassion.

6. Examine the stories you cling to.
The narratives we construct about our lives provide windows into formative experiences. What selective memories get recalled repeatedly as explanations or justifications for who you are and why you make certain choices? Recurring stories indicate unhealed wounds perpetuating those limited scripts.

7. Note childhood roles or identities.
Roles we took on as kids to feel safe often persist into adulthood, even when no longer adaptive. The "caretaker," "perfectionist," "loner," or "rebel" represent crystallized adaptations to childhood emotional wounds primed for healing.

By gently investigating these various clues, we can identify key memories and relationships that seem to disproportionately generate lasting pain and constraints on our sense of self.
These inquiries highlight wounds - but no judgement is needed.

Bring only compassionate curiosity to see what your psyche reveals.

Types of Memories to Explore

While singular traumatic events often shape us profoundly, emotional wounds need not be dramatic or obvious. More subtle but cumulative experiences of shame, betrayal, rejection, criticism, neglect, smothering, control, bullying and exclusion also carry powerful impacts, especially in childhood.

In fact, developmental psychologists find three periods especially formative for imprinting our lifelong emotional patterning:

1. Early childhood imprinting: Our primary caretakers' responses, attachments and attunement (or lack thereof) to our emotional needs shape our "working models" of self-worth and relational expectations profoundly from ages 0-5. Even preverbal events carry impact.

2. Major childhood transitions: Starting school, getting a new sibling, moving, divorces and other disruptions between ages 5-11 strongly influence our coping strategies, self-concept, and willingness to be vulnerable.

3. Adolescent identity integration: Intense neural, bodily, social and emotional changes challenge our sense of self and belonging between ages 12-18. Experiences of rejection, bullying, betrayal, failure, or disempowerment during this unstable time often generate lasting shame or insecurity.

While painful experiences likely occurred across all life stages, these developmental windows are ripe for excavating memories that became embedded foundationally into our neural nets and psyche. Because they shaped core attachment styles and traits while our brains were highly malleable, early memories carry particular potency for healing.

Additionally, look for patterns across similar hurts over time - not just singular episodes. Chronic dynamics of shame, control, bullying, or neglect become entrenched so gradually that we normalize them. Healing may require re-evaluating entire relationships, not just events.

Examples of Key Memories to Explore

To make these concepts more concrete, here are some examples of impactful memories to reflect on:

- A time of feeling deeply embarrassed, humiliated, rejected or misunderstood
- An incident of bullying, teasing, scapegoating or unfair punishment
- A betrayal of trust or grievous disappointment
- Witnessing acts of domestic violence or destructive conduct by parents.
- Emotionally abusive or chaotic households
- Attachment losses: deaths, abandonment, deployment, divorce

- Smothering parental control or impossible standards
- Sustained neglect or emotional absence
- Invalidating environments that denied, minimized or shamed feelings
- Persistent experiences of isolation, exclusion or lack of belonging
- Major losses in self-esteem such as getting fired or failed ambitions
- Disasters, accidents, violence requiring sudden adaptation

Use these categories as prompts to reflect deeply on your own history. Allow whatever arises to surface. Then, when ready, begin narrowing in on 2-3 specific memories for deeper exploration in the chapters ahead. These will serve as lenses into even broader relationship dynamics and social patterns that may require healing.

Guidance for Selecting Key Memories

As you sift through memories, consider the following markers to identify priority wounds for processing:

- Does reflecting on the memory still elicit strong or surprising emotions? Experiences we react to intensely years later indicate powerful neuronal patterning ready to be integrated.
- Did the event violate your sense of safety, trust or belonging at a core level? Incidents that ruptured fundamental security, especially in childhood, often distort our worldview most profoundly.

- Does the memory connect to any negative self-beliefs or ongoing behaviors? If current struggles with self-worth, depression, intimacy, or perfectionism have roots in a particular event, directly addressing that source memory will likely prove insightful.

- Is it a memory you intentionally avoid thinking about? Our minds often wall off what feels too painful to revisit. But suppressed memories exert unconscious control. Confronting avoided pain can be extremely liberating.

- Have you minimized the impact of this memory over time? We rationalize away many powerful memories as "not a big deal." But even small slights can imprint deeply on a child's mind. Consider fugitive memories with compassion.

- Does the memory remind you of unresolved aspects of your inner child that need healing? Our reactive emotions often reflect wounds of our younger self. Resolving the past heals present reactivity.

Identify 2-3 priority memories using these criteria - but don't overthink it. Even just 1-2 formative experiences harbor great potential for catalyzing integration. Our goal now is simply to highlight specific memories holding particular charge ready to be neutralized through compassionate understanding.

Integrating Key Memories into Your Consciousness

Having identified priority memories, take time in your journal to describe each in greater sensory and emotional detail. What images, scents, physical sensations, tastes or sounds do you associate with the event? What thoughts and emotions whirl through you when revisiting it? The brain integrates narrative memories more deeply when they are fleshed out holistically.

Don't judge this process or attempt to manage emotions that arise. Your only aim is to gently become reacquainted with hidden hurts long walled off for self-protection, welcoming them back into your consciousness so they can finally be laid to rest. By holding your own experiences and younger self with empathy, you begin shifting the energy of the memories themselves.

When ready, we will move to exercises for reframing these memories, updating their outdated interpretations, and permanently de-potentiating the fear and pain networks they activate. But for now, take time to open your awareness to suppressed hurts with radical self-compassion. Rather than demons to be slain, these wounds are teachers appearing when we're finally ready to receive their lessons in service of integration and growth. Honor the memories arising for the role they have played in your journey. Healing happens in layers. By courageously unearthing even just a few priority memories as gateway threads to pull, we unravel a lifetime's worth of hurt ready to transmute into hard-won wisdom.

Your psyche already knows exactly which experiences to reveal to initiate your most efficient healing. Trust its intelligence. Shift from avoidance to inquisitive excavation. Power awaits activation in your darkest recesses.

Chapter 3: How Negative Experiences Shape Your Thinking

In the previous chapters, we explored the general impacts of unresolved emotional wounds as well as how to identify priority memories for focused healing. Our next step in the journey is examining how those negative formative experiences actually imprint upon and alter our ways of thinking and filtering reality itself.

While time naturally dulls the intensity of any single memory, the narratives, beliefs, and neural associations formed in response to core hurts live on to shape our moment-to-moment perceptions, self-talk, and behaviors. Until we become aware of and intentionally rewrite the limiting mental frameworks formed around painful memories, they continue exerting quiet influence over our lives.

This chapter illuminates common thought patterns that crystallize around childhood emotional wounds. By recognizing unhelpful mental loops rooted in the past, we can loosen their grip and begin rewiring our brains toward more positive, empowering interpretations.

The Brain's Negativity Bias

To understand why our minds cling to negative interpretations requires first examining how human brains inherently function.

Across cultures, psychological research reveals most people exhibit a pronounced negativity bias - that is, the brain automatically prioritizes negative, threatening, or painful information over positive data.

Our primal wiring causes us to register negative experiences more strongly in memory because evolution conferred advantage to those focused on danger, lack, and pain. The human tendency to fixate on what's wrong far more than what's right served the critical purpose of survival for our ancestors.

However, this bias causes present difficulties by leading our minds to chronically and automatically interpret neutral or ambiguous situations through a negative lens. We reflexively pay more attention to criticism than praise, notice what's missing more than what's present, and recall failures more readily than successes.

When negative experiences in childhood coincide with the period our most formative neural wiring solidifies, this negativity bias gets locked in on overdrive. Painful memories shape our worldview disproportionately, generating lasting cognitive distortions that perpetuate suffering by maintaining a brain always primed for perceiving threats.

Common Cognitive Distortions

Decades of cognitive behavioral therapy research has revealed that most emotional suffering stems not from situations themselves, but rather from our interpretations of them. When childhood trauma skews our neural wiring towards habitual negativity, mature reality-testing capacity gets compromised.

In particular, cognitive therapists have identified 10 primary types of distorted thinking that emerge from painful early life experiences. See if you recognize any of these common cognitive distortions in your own mind:

1. **Black-or-white thinking** - Seeing in absolutes of "good/bad" with no nuance. Leads to harsh self-judgement.

2. **Overgeneralization** - Broad conclusions based on single events. Allows one failure to represent identity.

3. **Mental filter** - Dwelling on the negative and ignoring positive. Confirms own worst fears.

4. **Disqualifying the positive** - Rejecting praise, gifts, or achievements as undeserved or worthless. Deflects vulnerabilities of hope.

5. **Drawing premature conclusions** - Forming beliefs without substantiated proof. Assumes worst of behaviors or motives.

6. **Magnification and minimization** - Exaggerating negative impact while discounting positive events. Maximizes feelings of inadequacy.

7. **Emotional reasoning** - Treating negative emotions as facts. "I feel afraid so I must be in danger."

8. **Should statements** - Judging reality as it "should" be rather than how it is. Sets up expectations for disappointment.

9. **Labeling and mislabeling** - Broad terms like "I'm a loser" that become self-fulfilling.

10. **Personalization** - Taking the blame for external events.
Everything is interpreted as a personal referendum.

When we become aware of our own default cognitive distortions, we can challenge thought habits rooted in past pain that falsely confirm negative core beliefs about ourselves and the world. We gain power to rewrite mental narratives by exposing their logical fallacies.

Core Pain-Based Beliefs

Emotional wounds in childhood imprint not just in specific memories, but in the very lens through which we filter all subsequent experiences. In particular, research reveals core beliefs fall into three domains:

1. **Unlovability** - "I'm undesirable, unworthy, inadequate"
2. **Lack of trust** – "others will cause harm, betray, or abandon me."
3. **Helplessness** - "I have no control. Life is too hard."

These primal convictions generate downstream thoughts colored by themes of damage, distrust, defectiveness, disappointment, deprivation, disposability, imperfection, failure, or incompetence. Until core pain-based beliefs are brought to light with compassion, the mind automatically constructs stories confirming them as defense mechanisms. We continually recreate patterns of abandonment, rejection, shame, and punishment to align outside experiences with the inner narratives we know so well.

By consciously releasing these cognitive distortions, we reclaim power to shape new perspectives aligned with truths of our inherent worthiness, the basic goodness of others, and our capacity to cultivate joy.

Pain's Protective Logic

Importantly, the tendencies above emerged as necessary mental adaptations at the time of childhood wounds to cope with intolerable realities. When needs go chronically unmet or trauma shatters a child's sense of safety, control, and belonging, extreme judgments and perceptions feel rational. Believing "It's all my fault" or "No one can be trusted" reduces cognitive dissonance when a child lacks power to change home realities.

Later in adulthood when life conditions improve, these mental patterns persist, but they no longer serve us. In fact they generate unnecessary suffering by convincing us to expect and accept more pain.

By recognizing negative thought loops as legacies of old survival mechanisms run amuck, rather than inherent truths, we can dismantle them compassionately. The healing mind becomes able to perceive life's richness free from the veil of distortive filters.

Rewriting Mental Frameworks

Transforming mental frameworks shaped around childhood wounding requires four key steps:

1. **Identify automatic negative thoughts:** Start noticing self-critical inner voices, pessimistic interpretations, and bleak assumptions when they arise. Consider if any reflect common cognitive distortions that confirmation bias then solidifies as "truth."

2. **Link thoughts back to formative memories:** Ask yourself: "When was this core belief formed?" Tracing anxieties or negative narratives back to originating moments allows us to update limiting interpretations that crystallized long ago.

3. **Challenge negative thoughts with logic:** Talk back to negative voices, highlighting when thoughts magnify bad and minimize good, overgeneralize from single events, ignore nuance, or catastrophize possible outcomes. Insert realistic perspective.

4. **Rewrite narratives with compassion:** Rather than repressing negativity, dissolve old pain-based mental frameworks by composing affirmations of inherent worth, modeling self-talk on the wisdom of a trusted nurturing guide, and highlighting evidence that life supports rather than threatens you.

Incrementally releasing cognitive distortions through this process rewires neural associations, reduces habitual emotional reactivity, and empowers logical adult perspective to override the primal brain's fixed negativity bias.

In later chapters we'll explore practices to directly recalibrate neural networks through mindfulness, breathwork, and bilateral stimulation. But even just journaling to identify distorted thought patterns begins awakening us from trance-like automaticity. Noticing is healing.

Example Pain-Based Belief Examination

To make this process more concrete, let's walk through an example. Sam constantly struggles with thoughts like: "I'm such an idiot. I can't do anything right."

- **Identify automatic thoughts**: Self-judgement as "idiot," incompetent, inadequate.

- **Link to formative memories:** Sam traces this narrative back to memories of his father frequently calling him "useless" and "stupid" as a child when he made mistakes on household projects his dad forced him to help with.

- **Challenge with logic:** Sam now realizes his competence is average - these global labels overgeneralize. Everyone makes mistakes, but that doesn't negate their talents or deny their worth. His father's harsh criticism says more about dad's own insecurities.

- **Rewrite with compassion:** Sam counters the inner critic by affirming: "I have so many strengths and skills, even if I still make mistakes like anyone. I accept myself with loving kindness."

By methodically unraveling distortions rooted in Sam's father's emotional abuse, Sam stops perpetuating mental narratives that continue punishing his inner child in the present.

While recalibrating though patterns takes practice, it frees us from frames needlessly warping reality toward suffering. Our minds heal as we gently confront old belief systems crystallized from youthful survival logic that slanted perception darkly. But the light of awareness illuminates that in truth, we were worthy and lovable all along.

Chapter 4: Cultivating Self-Compassion and Self-Forgiveness

In the previous chapters, we explored how unhealed emotional wounds unconsciously shape our thoughts, behaviors, and identity. We also began the process of bringing formative painful memories into conscious awareness through practices of journaling, internal inquiry, and noticing habitual cognitive distortions.

Yet merely identifying our pain intellectually still keeps it at arm's length. To truly heal, we must shift from analysis to embodiment, and approach wounded parts of ourselves with the warmth of compassion rather than the cold lens of criticism.

This chapter provides exercises to help thaw the inner judge that often forms in response to childhood emotional neglect or trauma. By cultivating radical self-acceptance, we can finally integrate disowned aspects of our being and rewrite limiting narratives from a lens of wisdom, care, and forgiveness.

The Roots of Perfectionism

Many who experienced emotional wounds in childhood, particularly around achievement or meeting caregiver's expectations, develop troublesome perfectionistic traits that persist into adulthood. The inner critic emerges as an over-correction to perceived failure and feelings of unworthiness.

Perfectionism represents an attempt to reclaim control and prove worth through rigid self-discipline, sky high standards, and avoidance of mistakes. Of course, chasing perfect also guarantees perpetual disappointment. This generates a vicious shame cycle as we internalize the voice of parents or authorities who demanded excellence and punished missteps.

We avoid feelings of unlovability as long as we excel. But inwardly, the wounded child still yearns for unconditional positive regard. Healing involves cultivating self-love beyond metrics of achievement.

The Healing Power of Self-Compassion

To counteract hyper-critical tendencies, mindfulness research increasingly shows the immense benefits of self-compassion for emotional wellbeing. Whereas self-esteem rests on positive accomplishment, self-compassion radically accepts the whole self - flaws and failures included.

Self-compassion means bringing non-judgmental awareness to our own suffering and meeting it with the warmth we would extend to a dear friend struggling with the same issues. It provides emotional safety to feel, release, and integrate painful aspects of ourselves without compounding inner wounds through perfectionistic shame.

Studies confirm self-compassion builds resilience, reduces anxiety and depression, improves motivation, and enhances life satisfaction. It's also a key habit of the happiest, most emotionally intelligent people.

Importantly, self-compassion is not self-pity nor does it enable inertia. We remain accountable for growth. But we relate to ourselves as students, not adversaries. The inner mentor guides learning through encouragement, not punishment. With self-compassion, we can finally heal old emotional wounds because it is safe to be vulnerable.

Practicing Mindful Self-Compassion

Growing self-compassion involves both formal meditation and informal daily habits. Some starting practices include:

- **Soothing touch**. Place a hand gently on your heart, cheek, belly, or anywhere comforting. Feel the power of warmth and care. Send loving energy to tense areas. Repeat with regularity to re-pattern neural associations.

- **Lovingkindness meditation**. Generate positive emotions toward yourself and others repeating silent phrases like "May I be happy/healthy/peaceful/safe." Visualize someone you love enveloped in light. This conditions the mind for selfless compassion, soothing emotional reactivity.

- **Inner child dialogue**. Situate current struggles in the experience of your younger self. Imagine that child with compassion. Offer perspective from your wiser adult self through journaling. "You did the best you could then. I accept you now just as you are."

- **Self-acceptance Mantras**. Compose positive affirmations countering the critic. Let the statements soothe rather than suppress pain. "I wholeheartedly embrace myself in the present moment" "I am sufficient," "My value is not determined by accomplishment." Repeat as affirmations to reframe self-concept.

- **Change negative self-talk**. Notice critical inner voices. Gently talk back with compassion for yourself. "It's okay to make mistakes! You are in the process of learning." Recognizing your inner voice is the initial stage of softening it.

- **Self-forgiveness**. Through meditation or writing, consciously release shame, regret or self-blame for past actions. Accept that you acted from your level of awareness at the time. Commit to growth without guilt. We are all imperfect beings being worked on.

- **Normalize failure**. No one is perfect or hardship-free. Remember you are part of the shared human experience. Failure is part of growth. Allow grace through difficulties.

Regularly taking time to care for yourself with the gentleness, understanding and nurturing you would extend to dearest loved ones gradually unravels tendencies of self-flagellation rooted in childhood emotional wounds. Your spirit thrives in the light of self-compassion.

Rewriting Core Shame-Based Beliefs

Perfectionistic inner critics often emerge in response to implicit core beliefs of unworthiness, inadequacy or shame carried over from childhood. By identifying and rewriting those deep rooted mental frameworks, we disrupt critical commentary at its source.

Through journaling, bring non-judgmental awareness to beliefs like:

- I'm worthless/inadequate unless I achieve

- I'm unlovable when I make mistakes

- I'm defective so must hide imperfections

- I deserve criticism for failing

- If I don't criticize myself, no one else will

- I cannot handle disapproval so must be perfect

- I'm an imposter. If people really knew me, they would be repulsed

- I'm stupid/bad for having needs or feelings

Meet these inner convictions with empathy. Recognize they arose to protect a vulnerable younger self trying to navigate impossible situations. Then slowly unravel them by writing new, wise, compassionate narratives. For example:

- Mistakes do not define my worth or lovability

- I accept and love myself unconditionally

- I allow myself to be imperfect and human

- My best is always enough. Growth, not perfection, is the goal

- I approve of myself exactly as I am in this moment

- All people have intrinsic dignity and beauty

- I compassionately accept all parts of my being

Keep paragraphs short and emotionally resonant. Repeat these revised belief statements regularly. Support with loving affirmations and behaviors. In time, self-acceptance grows.

The Neuroscience of Self-Compassion

Recent neuroscience research reveals fascinating details about how self-compassion heals the wounded heart and mind at a biological level:

- Soothing touch and caring behaviors release oxytocin, quieting the body's stress response. Feelings of safely and peace expand.

- Activating the parasympathetic nervous system through breathing, yoga, or meditation balances out fight-or-flight excess, reducing anxiety and perfectionistic overdrive.

- Labeling negative self-talk in an unbiased way disempowers it by decreasing amygdala reactivity in the emotional brain. Pain loses its grip.

- Focused compassion practices light up neural networks for empathy while deactivating parts of the brain that generate shame, fear or anger. Emotional wisdom grows.
- Over time, decreased threat sensitivity and fear conditioning from self-compassion reshape neural structures away from states of constant hypervigilance, irritation, or defensiveness. Patience and clarity blossom.

In essence, caring for oneself with daily compassion meditation, mantras, journaling, and supportive mental reframing creates a brain chemistry of emotional safety, soothing cellular inflammation and anxiety. Neural pathways elevating gentleness then reinforce themselves through neuroplastic change.

While never easy, committing to self-compassion promises deep healing. Your mind releases suffocating expectations when it recognizes you were already whole all along.

Integrating the Inner Critic with Radical Self-Acceptance

Importantly, the goal of self-compassion is not to banish the inner critic entirely, which would create new inner conflict. Attempting to suppress any part of ourselves only breeds psychic unrest.

For sustainable change, we make space for all voices within us with loving wisdom. The critic simply becomes integrated as one limited perspective, no longer dominating as a tyrant. We relate to our perfectionism with interest instead of rejection.

Radically accepting all aspects of ourselves defangs shame. We hold imperfections, struggles and pain with warm hands - as teachers instead of enemies. Parts wishing we were different relax at last in the relief that we need not earn existence or love. They come just for being.

This work of nourishing inner peace asks much: determined compassion towards those who harmed us, those we harmed, and most of all, to ourselves. But by Gelfand to befriend all that arises within us, we reduce the compulsion to achieve, grasp, avoid, or attach our worth to fleeting conditions. In stillness, we are already sacred.

May you come home to yourself.

Chapter 5: Learning to Let Go Through Mindfulness

Up to this point, we've focused primarily on identifying and understanding the impacts of painful childhood memories as well as common thought distortions that may have crystallized around formative wounds.

Bringing this intellectual awareness to our hurt parts is the vital first step to healing. But to fully release the hold past trauma exerts requires directly working with difficult emotions through the practice of mindfulness.

Mindfulness means gently bringing non-judgmental attention to your moment-to-moment experience. It enables us to witness even intense discomfort with curiosity and care instead of avoidance. Learning to stay grounded when emotional storms arise empowers us to understand, respect, and gradually diffuse lingering wounds.

This chapter provides essential mindfulness techniques to help you cultivate acceptance of painful sensations, unhook from unhelpful thought loops, and relate to memories from your wise adult self rather than wounded inner child. Equanimity grows the more we hold our experiences with open hands instead of clenched fists.

Why Mindfulness Facilitates Healing

Mindfulness works to loosen the grip of past trauma in several key ways:

- **It builds distress tolerance.** Rather than being overwhelmed when challenging emotions like anger, grief, or shame surface, mindfulness helps us remain grounded enough to meet their arising with equanimity. We learn we can handle discomforts, which dissolves avoidance.

- **It increases response flexibility.** Mindfulness creates a pause between an emotion arising and our habitual reactive patterns. This gap allows us to consciously choose skillful responses aligned with values rather than acting from trauma-based conditioning.

- **It promotes self-compassion.** Observing ourselves with kind curiosity enables us to extend empathy towards our own wounds and struggles. We hold pain with care rather than exacerbate it with criticism.

- **It enhances emotional intelligence.** As we become familiar with the sensations and dynamics of various emotions, we gain emotional literacy to skillfully navigate their currents. We understand the nature rather than rejecting the content.

- **It facilitates neuroplasticity**. Regular mindfulness literally changes the structure and functioning of the brain over time, strengthening neural pathways that downregulate reactivity, fear, and rumination while boosting capacities for emotional wisdom.

In essence, mindfulness is the light that illuminates the unconscious forces driving our suffering. By patiently training awareness on inner experiences, we unravel ingrained mental and emotional patterns shaped around old pain. Equanimity dispels distortions.

Establishing a Daily Mindfulness Practice

Just like physical exercise, mindfulness requires regular practice to reap benefits. Start by establishing a formal sitting meditation habit, even if only 5-10 minutes daily. Find a quiet space, close your eyes, and bring non-judgmental awareness to:

- Sounds - Notice all the distinct nearby and distant sounds without getting hooked on narrative meanings. Let them come and go.
- Physical sensations - Tune into the breath and subtle bodily sensations without trying to change them. Note areas of tightness or relaxation.
- Thoughts - Observe thoughts like clouds passing in the sky without grabbing onto them. Release rather than ruminate.

- Emotions - Allow any feelings arising to be there without suppressing or exaggerating them. Meet their presence with gentle curiosity.

The key is not to force any change or deep spiritual experience. Simply practice returning again and again to an anchor of present moment sensory awareness whenever the mind gets pulled into stories and analysis. Patient dedication to regrounding in your body breeds calm abiding presence.

In addition to formal sits, aim to weave mindful embodiment into your daily life. Some easy ways include:

- Mindful eating - Savoring food textures and flavors

- Mindful walking or hiking - Feeling the feet on the ground

- Mindful driving - Noticing sensations of motion

- Mindful waiting - Feeling the breathe rather than grabbing your phone at every idle moment

- Mindful listening - Giving your full presence to someone speaking

- Mindful transitions - Pausing to take 3 conscious breaths when your activity changes

Get creative identifying simple ways to inject mindfulness into mundane moments to continually connect to the anchor of the here and now. Each instance of presence strengthens neural circuitry for regulating distress.

Working With Difficult Emotions Mindfully

Once you've established a consistent mindfulness practice through focusing on neutral sensory experiences as described above, you can apply presence to work with challenging emotional states:

- **Name it**. Note when anger, fear, grief, shame, or other feelings you typically avoid arise. Dispassionately label the emotion you're experiencing without judgment or rejection.

- **Allow it**. Let the emotional energy fully be there without trying to cling to it or push it away. Breathe into any tension around it in your body. Fighting a feeling only magnifies it.

- **Feel it**. Pay close attention to the physical, muscular, and postural components of the emotion. What are its subtle qualities? Meet its intensity with gentle curiosity.

- **Non-identify**. Remember that you are not the emotion itself, but the awareness witnessing it come and go like a wave. No feeling defines you or makes you lose control.

- **Speak to it**. Have an inner conversation with the emotion, validating its presence, hearing its messages, but setting boundaries if its expressions become destructive. See it as information rather than enemy.

- **Let it evolve**. Observe how emotional energy naturally morphs when fully allowed rather than suppressed. Note how even intense anger or grief dissipates in time if simply observed.

- **Take mindful action**. Reflect on skillful choices for working with the emotion and meeting underlying needs. Speak your truth, get support, or problem solve. Mindful action reduces rumination.

By welcoming even painful or frightening inner states with compassion and courage through mindfulness, their grip over us gradually dissolves. We cease being a victim to reactivity, reclaiming power to respond from emotional wisdom.

Using Mindfulness to Rewrite Trauma Narratives

In addition to building equanimity around intense emotions, mindfulness helps rewrite limiting narratives formed around childhood memories.

Rather than remaining fused with the perspective of your past self when reliving old wounds, mindfulness enables us to compassionately witness memories from the wise, emotionally regulated space of the adult self in the present.

Try this "rewind" practice:

1. Close your eyes and re-imagine yourself back in a painful childhood memory. See the scene through your younger eyes once again. Notice the associated thoughts, emotions and body sensations that arise.

2. Now, float out of the memory to watch things unfold as an objective, compassionate observer. See your younger self there with empathy. Send love.

3. Rewind the memory and watch it again, intervening with any wisdom or comfort as your adult self. Picture offering resources and reassurance to the child.

4. Affirm that the challenging experience is now over and that you emerged resilient. Soothing energy integrates knowing you survived and thrived.

This exercise of revisiting memories with mindful presence lets us consciously process pain through the lens of acquired maturity rather than raw childhood emotion. We hold our suffering from long ago with care, separating past from present. The neural pathways encoding victimhood transform. We are no longer trapped in the past.

Common Mindfulness Pitfalls

Like any skill, mindfulness takes patience and practice. Take notice of these typical mistakes made by beginners:

- Trying too hard to empty the mind or attain special states - Simply practice relaxed, open awareness without expectations or force.

- Using mindfulness to suppress emotions - Allow them to move through rather than restrict flow. Suppression just represses.

- Self-criticizing when the mind inevitably wanders - Redirecting attention is the practice. Return with self-compassion.

- Zone out dullness rather than sharp presence - Keep the mind energized yet mellow. Adjust posture or splash cold water if tired.

- Practicing only when calm - Apply mindfulness precisely when stressed or triggered. Those rough moments hold the most power for change.

- Observing emotions intellectually without feeling - Don't distance from discomfort. Lean in to truly release trauma stored in the body.

- Skipping daily practice - Consistency compounds benefits over time as mental grooves deepen. Prioritize just a few minutes if busy.

Mindfulness works when done regularly with an attitude of engaged, compassionate curiosity towards reality just as it is - not ideally how we wish it was. By repeatedly touching experience nakedly beyond conceptual filters, we reconnect to joy's hum of belonging to life in each moment.

Crystallizing Gains Through Lovingkindness Practice

To help positive mindfulness states permeate your daily consciousness, end meditations by visualizing compassion radiating outward through the following lovingkindness practice:

May I be healthy.

May I be peaceful.

May I live with ease.

May I live with joy.

Gradually expand this heartfelt wish outward:

To loved ones...

To neutrals...

To those causing harm...

To all beings everywhere...

These ancient phrases condition your mind to extend unconditional goodwill to all, including towards yourself - countering self-criticism. Send ribbons of care into your day.

By repeatedly grounding in mindful embodiment when emotional storms arise, we relate to even painful memories with poise instead of panic. We need no longer be at the mercy of imprinted trauma when mindfulness empowers us to compassionately hold our experiences while trusting in our essential okay-ness.

As one Zen teaching reminds, "Let everything happen to you: beauty and terror. Just keep going. No feeling is final."

Chapter 6: Rewriting Your Narrative and Reframing the Past

Up until this point, we've focused primarily on building mindfulness skills to develop equanimity when confronting painful memories and emotions. By improving our capacity for compassionate inner awareness, we've created the proper mental environment to now begin actively processing formative wounds to finally release their hold.

The practices in this chapter move beyond just observing difficult memories and into directly reframing their meaning through cognitive reappraisal techniques rooted in leading therapies like Cognitive Behavioral Therapy (CBT), Neuro-Linguistic Programming (NLP), and Internal Family Systems (IFS).

Whereas mindfulness strengthened our ability to remain even-keeled within emotional storms, targeted reappraisal enables us to permanently calm the weather itself by revising disempowering scripts encoded in implicit memory. We're no longer passive recipients of traumatic imprinting, but active participants in rewriting our life narratives.

The Power of Cognitive Reframing

Decades of psychotherapy research reveals our perceptions of events themselves, more than any objective facts, shape the meaning we unconsciously attribute to past experiences. Challenging engrained neural frameworks that crystalized around childhood trauma opens space for new perspectives to emerge.

Reframing does not necessarily mean replacing dark perceptions with naively positive illusions. Instead, through a process of questioning inherent beliefs, assumptions and assigned meanings within memories, we restore nuance and context to find glimmers of insight within the pain.

The reflexive narratives and worldviews shaped by past wounds lose their vise-grip as we identify self-protective but ultimately limiting ways of interpreting what happened to us. We reconnect to truth rather than trauma.

Noticing vs. Changing Thoughts

Importantly, reframing builds upon the mindfulness practices covered earlier for emotional regulation. We first develop the ability to compassionately notice thoughts before endeavoring to alter them. Attempting to manipulate thoughts through force of will often breeds inner conflict or repression. Such control stems from ego rather than wisdom.

Instead, reframing works organically once mindfulness helps us detach enough to observe even painful thought patterns with calm curiosity. We create space for clarity to emerge.

Equanimity around our inner experiences must precede efforts to actively change them. Reframing grounded in mindfulness opens us to truth rather than imposes narrative.

Steps for Reframing Painful Memories

With that understanding, the process of reappraising traumatic memories involves:

1. **Revisiting:** Begin by purposefully yet calmly recalling a painful memory. See it vividly in your mind's eye. Notice associated thoughts, emotions and body sensations.

2. **Evaluating:** Consider the assumed meanings, projections, judgments, conclusions, or core beliefs you unconsciously attached to this memory over time. Does it confirm narratives of unworthiness, guilt, or defectiveness? How so?

3. **Questioning:** Pose thoughtful questions to unravel the memories' assigned significance. Does it really imply what you assumed? Recognize projections. Could other benign meanings be equally valid? What broader context is missing?

4. **Reflecting:** Based on your questioning, summarize any distorted interpretations you now notice. How did the mind warp, exaggerate, or filter the memory to reinforce limiting self-concepts? What meanings actually feel true vs. protective illusions?

5. **Reframing:** Finally, intentionally re-encode the memory with more expansive understanding. Highlight lessons or opportunities for growth the past offers in present wisdom. Find empathy for yourself. Edit old scripts.

6. **Reconsolidating:** Review your reframed insights regularly so they become familiar neural patterns that weaken outdated trauma mindsets through neuroplasticity. Your relationship with the memory organically shifts.

While often challenging, examining formative memories with radical self-honesty and compassion ultimately liberates us from their distortive grip on our sense of identity and possibility. We reclaim authorship over our inner narratives.

Questions to Facilitate Reframing

Here are sample self-inquiry questions to explore when working to reframe specific memories:

- Is there any evidence contradicting the negative meanings I've assigned?

- How might other people interpret this same event positively?

- What feelings or unmet needs might have fueled others' harmful behaviors toward me? (understanding enhances forgiveness)

- How did social/cultural factors contribute nuance to the situation?

- Did I perceive any threat or malice that wasn't actually present?

- How did my own expectations shape my interpretations?

- What are the smallest signs of growth or redemption within the experience?

- What lessons or strengths did I gain by enduring this challenge?

- How did focusing on this memory distort my beliefs about myself or worldview in unreasonable ways?

- How would I advise a dear friend to reframe this situation with wisdom and care?

- What meaning could I assign to expand my dated understandings and see things more holistically?

As your automatic trauma perceptions defrost, radical acceptance and new possibility emerge.

Reframing Your Core Wound

To make memory reappraisal feel more concrete, let's walk through a personal example:

When Sara was 11, her father abandoned the family unexpectedly without explanation. Young Sara concluded his leaving meant she was unworthy of love. This core wound shaped a restrictive belief that she was too flawed for commitment.

In adulthood, she realized this belief sabotaged relationships and fueled abandonment fears. She revisited the memory with intention to reframe its meaning.

- **Revisiting:** What images, feelings and assumptions arise when recalling dad's leaving?

- **Evaluating:** I assumed it meant I was defective. This seeded an identity as unlovable.

- **Questioning:** Did being abandoned really imply that about me or say more about dad's issues? If friends were in this situation, would I say they were unworthy of love?

- **Reflecting:** The meaning I assigned was an exaggerated, self-protective narrative of a scared child. It became a limited filter.

- **Reframing:** While dad's actions were deeply painful, I now know my worth and lovability are unconditional. His choice reflected his struggles, not mine. This experience helped me cultivate resilience and empathy for others experiencing loss.

- **Reconsolidating:** When abandonment fears arise, I remind myself of my reframed understanding of this memory. My core wound has transformed into a source of strength.

While Sara's father's actions still hurt, reframing the meaning of this key trauma liberated her from its involuntary emotional control. Your memories await similar alchemy.

Additional Reframing Practices

In addition to self-inquiry questioning, the following exercises can aid reframing efforts:

- **Mindful self-dialogue:** Imagining a wise inner mentor gently challenging your trauma assumptions creates new neurological pathways. Practice having this imaginary mentor guide you toward more empowered narratives.

- **Lovingkindness meditation:** Cultivating warm feelings of compassion toward yourself, even in relation to your darkest memories, dissolves harmful beliefs of unworthiness or deficiency reinforced during past trauma.

- **Gratitude:** Actively searching for any learning, growth, resilience or insight garnered from past pain softens memories by highlighting hidden gifts within the grief. Be creative looking for sources of gratitude.

- **Artistic processing:** Painting, drawing, dancing, singing or writing about a memory from a place of present wisdom often reveals liberating new emotional dimensions. Get intuitive.

- **Somatic therapy:** Methods like EMDR leverage bilateral stimulation to reprocess memories at a neural level beyond intellectual narratives. Seek trained guidance to unlock stored emotional energy in the body-mind.

- **Inner child work:** Dialoguing with, visualizing or writing compassionate letters to your younger wounded self shifts perspective to realize you were doing your best given limited resources. Core wounds transform from tales of damage into accounts of courage.

However, you choose to engage them, relating to your memories as living fluid processes rather than frozen artifacts allows their outdated meanings to evolve with the wisdom you've accumulated. The past gently integrates.

Chapter 7: Tapping Into Post-Traumatic Growth

Up to this point, we've covered various techniques for developing self-awareness, cultivating mindfulness, practicing self-compassion, and reframing fixed narratives around your most painful past memories. With dedication and courage, you've created space for long-suppressed hurts to finally be addressed skillfully. Yet essential to the journey is realizing that processing trauma is not solely about closing wounds, but opening access to new sources of meaning, purpose, and capability that could not take root without the fertile soil forged through adversity.

This chapter explores the pioneering concept of post-traumatic growth: how crisis, struggle, and suffering inevitably sow the seeds for profound transformation when met with bravery, meaning-making, and intentional growth. By realizing the wisdom and gifts birthed even from life's most difficult chapters, we become the authors of our own redemption.

Understanding Post-Traumatic Growth

The notion of post-traumatic growth emerged fairly recently in psychology through the pioneering research of psychologists like Richard Tedeschi, Lawrence Calhoun, and others.

It encapsulates the curious paradox that human beings often derive immense strengths, growth, insight, improved relationships, deepened spirituality, and renewed appreciation for life as the long-term result of grappling with trauma, crisis, illness, loss, violence, or other adversities.

While the process of healing from hardship is slow and painful, those who do the work of metabolizing experiences in the forge of courage and meaning often emerge on the other side fundamentally changed in positive ways that would have remained dormant without the catalyst of crisis.

Studies show these kinds of transformative post-traumatic outcomes include:

- Increased resilience, emotional intelligence, wisdom
- Improved connections, vulnerability, compassion
- Strengthened sense of meaning, purpose, self-efficacy
- Shift to prioritizing growth over safety
- Hope and optimism about the future
- Enhanced spirituality and contemplative ability
- Renewed gratitude, presence, appreciation for life

In essence, darkness leads to light. Suffering faced squarely with honesty, intention, and support breaks open untapped reservoirs of human potential. Hardship becomes healing when reframed as an initiation.

The Paradox of Emotional Wounds

Importantly, recognizing the opportunities hidden within your most painful memories does not imply trauma itself is ever beneficial or that victims are responsible for extracting positives. Suffering is never justified or deserved.

Rather, growth occurs not because adversity is good, but because the human spirit defiantly calls forward redemption from even life's bleakest chapters. We courageously ascribe meaning to rise like a phoenix from the ashes of misfortune.

It is precisely our core human capacities to search for wisdom, cultivate compassion, foster connection, and rewrite narratives that allow us to turn emotional wounds from tales of damage into accounts of courage.

By engaging trauma with radical intention, presence, and meaning-making, we turn lead into gold, poison into medicine. It is an astounding testament to human resilience.

Myths & Misconceptions

Before exploring how to cultivate post-traumatic growth (PTG) in your own life, it's useful to dispel some common myths and misconceptions about this concept:

- **PTG is not universal** - Not all people will experience growth. It depends on willingness for self-work.

- **PTG is not a quick fix** – It unfolds gradually through ongoing courage and intention.

- **PTG is not a cure for trauma** – Wounds may still linger. But their impact transforms.

- **PTG is not a comparison game** - Each person's growth is unique. No need to judge your journey.

- **PTG does not imply victim blaming** – Responsibility lies solely with perpetrators of harm.

- **PTG does not erase pain** – Grief still arises amid growth. The two coexist.

Understanding both the power and parameters of post-traumatic growth allows us to realistically harness it without minimizing the need for continued healing. Growth flows alongside ongoing inner work.

Domains of Post-Traumatic Growth

Researchers who study PTG note recurring areas of positive change frequently reported by trauma survivors. Consider if any of the domains below resonate with your own experience:

- **Greater appreciation for life** – Renewed gratitude for each day can emerge from glimpsing mortality. Small joys become miracles.

- **Deepened spirituality** – Trauma often opens portals to the sacred and ignites existential questioning that enhances faith or purpose.

- **Improved relationships** – Shared suffering fosters empathy and dissolving masks to create mutual bonds of authenticity.

- **Increased personal strength** – Successfully enduring adversity breeds durable self-efficacy and courage to withstand future challenges. What doesn't break you has the potential to fortify you.

- **Positive changes in self-concept** – Healing instills greater compassion, vulnerability, acceptance and emotional intelligence.

- **New possibilities** – Loss and tragedy disrupt old limiting narratives and make space for new growth-oriented meaning.

- **Enhanced appreciation for mortality** – Visceral understanding that life is fleeting shifts priorities toward cherishing each moment.

Consider if any of these common areas of positive change parallel your own post-traumatic insights. But also allow any unique experiences of growth to emerge. There are countless paths to transformation.

Practices to Cultivate Post-Traumatic Growth

With this understanding of common PTG domains, here are some reflective practices you can engage to begin consciously anchoring growth:

- **Gratitude journaling** – Regularly record moments of appreciation, meaning, blessings, affection, beauty, joy, love, or transformation. This magnifies positives blossoming alongside lingering hurts.

- **Revisit assumptions** – Consider how trauma may have shattered limiting beliefs about yourself, others, or life that now allows you to see things more accurately. Update rigid narratives.

- **Foster supportive community** – Find those who facilitate healing through non-judgment, guidance, and safe vulnerability. Positive relationships magnify growth.

- **Uncover hidden gifts** – Explore how exactly crisis equipped you with new abilities like resilience, wisdom, self-knowledge, empathy or purpose you can now carry forward.

- **Engage in altruism** – Find opportunities to use your experiences to help others undergoing similar situations. Aid them to transform vicarious pain into virtue.

- **Create meaning** – Through journaling, art, conversation, or spiritual practices, explore how exactly your hardship catalyzed intimations of what matters most to you or a clarified sense of purpose.

- **Develop rituals** – Symbolically acknowledge periods of transition from trauma to growth through ceremonies marking changed understandings of self and world.

- **Imagine possibilities** – Envision how emerging strengths, priorities, values, and identities create space for higher quality relationships, work, creativity, and inner peace after healing.

- **Forgive constructively** – Consider carefully offering judicious forgiveness to those who caused harm, not to minimize damage but to acknowledge how even unjust suffering cultivates wisdom when met with courage.

By proactively engaging such practices, you consecrate wounds as fertile ground for cultivating post-traumatic strengths and meaning. Shift perspective from *"victim of circumstance"* to *"student of experience."* Each instance of awareness around growth also rewards the brain, further solidifying helpful neural patterns that reinforce resilience.

In time, your relationship to past pain transforms. Tragedies lose their destructive power in the light of how they propelled you toward deeper purpose and poise. You recast your life story from one of damage to redemption.

Integration: A Lifelong Process

Keep in mind that post-traumatic growth is an ongoing process rather than a single moment of epiphany. New layers of learning and insight about your experiences will continue surfacing over time.

It is not that grief ever disappears entirely. More so that glimmers of wisdom make suffering bearable, even purposeful. Dark nights of the soul may come and go. But your values, priorities, and self-concept remain irrevocably changed.

Respond to each stage of positive change as a chapter in your unfolding story - inseparable mixtures of both suffering and liberation. Poignancy and peace coexist when we realize everything belongs exactly as it is, became we became who we are because of it.

All of the pain, all of the beauty - fused in wisdom to write the next line of the epic poem that is your precious human life. Keep growing.

Chapter 8: Establishing Boundaries to Protect Your Peace

We come now to the final phase of our journey together exploring strategies to compassionately understand, process and release childhood emotional wounds to step into greater freedom and possibility.

In the previous chapters, we covered powerful practices including identifying core memories, cultivating mindfulness, reframing stories, and discovering post-traumatic growth. With courage and care, you've created space for old hurts to integrate and transform. Yet given the deep roots of formative pain, dedicated ongoing cultivation is required to ensure new wisdom and strengths crystallize moving forward. Unconscious patterns persist out of habit until intentionally dismantled through mindful action.

This chapter offers essential guidance on establishing healthy proactive boundaries and behaviors to protect your emerging peace, integrate lessons learned, and prevent sliding backwards into past wounded thinking and reactions.

The Process of Creating New Neural Patterns

Thanks to neuroplasticity - the brain's ability to continually form new neural connections in response to experiences - practicing the self-work and embodiment exercises covered in this book physically alter neural wiring over time.

Consciously focusing attention on breath, body sensations, and non-judgmental awareness of thoughts and emotions strengthens neural pathways for safety, equanimity and emotional regulation.

Likewise, intentionally reframing memories and beliefs with radical self-honesty and self-compassion creates fresh neuronal patterns encoding healthier perspectives. The dense tangle of fear-based trauma thinking gradually unwinds.

However, because our default programming still contains millions of well-worn reactive pathways ready to reignite, success requires ongoing diligence and care. To consciously sculpt new neural patterns requires insulating against habit's gravity.

We must compassionately yet firmly protect our peace, recognizing attempts of wounded ego patterns to re-form and pull us backwards. But self-care is not about perfection. It is about continually returning to wisdom when we temporarily forget - which itself further ingrains desired paths.

Managing Pain Triggers

A primary way we sustain positive changes is by managing situations likely to catalyze traumatic emotional flashbacks and pull us back into wounded thinking.

Start by identifying your common triggers - experiences that reliably destabilize your sense of safety and equilibrium when they echo old pain patterns.

For instance, common triggers include:

- Interactions with certain toxic personalities
- Visiting dysfunctional home environments
- Self-criticism and perfectionism
- Social rejection or romantic disappointments
- Overwork and lack of self-care
- Social media exposure to others' curated lives
- News coverage of trauma and adversity

Make a list of your pain triggers across different life domains - relationships, work, health, media consumption. Remember that because triggers unconsciously activate your threat response and limbic system's negativity bias, they distort perspective by making neutral situations seem dangerous.

Once you have awareness of common triggers, you can take proactive steps to thoughtfully manage exposure:

- Limit time with personalities that destabilize you
- Practice self-care if returning home
- Reframe inner criticism mindfully
- Allow space to grieve losses through journaling
- Set boundaries around work hours
- Unfollow accounts prompting social comparison
- Limit unnecessary news consumption

The goal is not total avoidance, but moderating exposure to what we know overactivates our traumatized nervous system pending further healing. Stay mindful of triggers, but respond skillfully without self-blame if they arise.

Self-Care to Optimize Mental Wellbeing

Ongoing loving self-care is essential to reinforce the nascent neural patterns holding your emerging emotional wisdom. Fortify inner peace by proactively:

- **Prioritizing daily meditation** to strengthen equanimity. Even a few minutes makes a difference.
- **Getting sufficient sleep** for optimal mind-body health. Protect sleep hygiene.
- **Eating nutritious foods** to stabilize energy, mood, and cognition. Hydrate well.
- **Exercising** for mental clarity, stress relief, and mood boosts through natural endorphins.
- **Cultivating nature time** for perspective on what truly matters and to reduce anxiety.
- **Enjoying relaxing hobbies** that connect you to pleasure and flow. Make time for joy.
- **Engaging in social connection** for support, meaning, and to counteract isolation.
- **Seeking therapy** if needed to process deeper issues safely with a pro.

Make self-care non-negotiable just as you would manage any health condition. You deserve to feel peaceful and well. Protect your energy.

Maintaining an Inner Practice

Complement daily self-care with a regular inner practice that sustains the gains made in equanimity, self-compassion and conscious thinking.

Choose a mindfulness, meditation, journaling, or contemplative ritual that suits your personality. Some options include:

- **Daily meditation** to remain anchored in presence free from reactive thoughts.
- **Lovingkindness practice** to continually condition feelings of warmth towards yourself and others.
- **Gratitude journaling** to maintain perspective on blessings and positive changes unfolding.
- **Creative expression** through art, music, dance to process and integrate memories through right-brained flow.
- **Counseling or support groups** to discuss ongoing challenges in a spirit of vulnerability.
- **Reading books** on topics of inner growth, mindfulness, self-compassion or resilience.
- **Spending time in nature** to access peace and stillness.
- **Contemplative walking** to integrate learning through rhythmic embodied movement.

Choose practices that feel energizing and centering rather than depleting. The goal is sustaining psycho-emotional stamina. Make time for inner work, not just outer achievement.

Relating Skillfully to Residual Pain

Importantly, as we shed layers of historical hurt, some measure of grief, anger or shame may continue surfacing situationally. This is a typical occurrence and should not be seen as a sign of failure. Relate to residual emotions without self-blame when they inevitably arise by:

- Noticing and naming them mindfully without judgement
- Allowing them space to move through awareness
- Utilizing tools like deep breathing, grounding, mantras to self-soothe
- Understanding they are just transitory echoes of past pain arising to finish processing
- Appreciating their appearance as a sign you are sensitively thawing old numbness
- Reaffirming core truths of inherent worth, belonging, and impermanence
- Reacting to any triggers skillfully without self-criticism

Healing is cyclical, not linear. Temporary emotional flare-ups are like forest fires clearing way for new growth. Meet residual pain with self-compassion, not self-attack.

Conclusion: A New Chapter Begins

Although inner work is ever-unfolding, take time to honor closure of this focused healing phase by consciously noting the changes sprouting from suffering transmuted.

Celebrate evidence of post-traumatic growth in your increased empathy, equanimity, wisdom, purpose and peace. Appreciate how even the deepest wounds tilled soil for new discovery.

While shadows of pain may organically arise at times, you no longer reside at the mercy of suffering. Emotional education has dawned. Scattered pieces now form beautiful mosaic.

Yet also know that your learning journey is never truly complete. Allow this ending to become a hopeful new beginning. Take courage and keep growing, just as a wise oak continues reaching upward throughout the seasons, patiently adding rings of character with each cycle of life.

You are the narrator of your own heroic journey. Write each next chapter with self-compassion and grace. The pen is in your hands. Onward...

Chapter 9: Filling Your Life with Purpose and Meaning

We now arrive at the final stop on our shared journey of understanding emotional wounds and learning practices to compassionately process, integrate, and release their hold to step into greater freedom and possibility.

In the previous chapters, we explored powerful tools to develop self-awareness, rewrite limiting narratives, cultivate mindfulness, and initiate transformations of post-traumatic growth.

Yet inner work cannot simply be about recovering from the past. True healing propels us forward to intentionally create lives of purpose and meaning that honor our struggles by fully embodying hard-won wisdom every day.

This chapter offers guidance on mindfully filling your present with pursuits that light you up from the inside out - activities expressive of your values, passions, and new identity detached from past pain.

The key is no longer allowing emotional wounds to overly shape your decisions and behaviors reactively. Instead, with mindfulness, choose life-affirming actions aligned with your authentic inner compass.

Clarifying Your Values

Values are your heart's deepest desires for how you want to interact with the world - what truly matters to you. They symbolize your dreams and priorities.

Start by brainstorming a list of words or phrases that resonate with you. Common values include:

- Integrity, authenticity, honesty
- Learning, growth, creativity
- Community, connection, belonging
- Justice, equality, ethics
- Beauty, wonder, joy
- Peace, presence, mindfulness
- Compassion, service, generosity
- Health, wellness, thriving
- Freedom, independence, liberation
- Fun, humor, playfulness

Reflect on which values energize you and guide your choices. How would you love to experience life and relate to others?

Then periodically check in during daily decisions: "Does this action align with my values?" Consciously choosing value-based behaviors builds meaning.

Clarifying Your Priorities

Next, within your identified values, reflect on specific life domains you want to prioritize:

- **Relationships** – How do you wish to connect with others moving forward from your healed space? What boundaries or communication habits will serve your growth?

- **Career** – Does your work allow you to express your authentic gifts and passions? If not, consider how to pivot toward more meaning.

- **Wellbeing** – Are you prioritizing self-care such as healthy habits, body movement, and mind-body practices? These fortify healing.

- **Personal Growth** – How will you continue challenging yourself to learn, create, expand perspective, and actualize potentials?

- **Leisure** – Are you making time for hobbies, experiences and adventures that spark joy and wonder? Play nourishes the soul.

- **Spirituality** – Do you feel connected to something larger than the self? If not, try cultivating awe in nature, meditation, or community.

- **Contribution** – Volunteering, mentoring and service activities who share your gifts make life purposeful. Offer your learning to the world.

Take inventory of which domains feel balanced or neglected. Then set intentions for any areas requiring more attention.

Discovering Meaningful Activities

With clarified values and priorities, now envision tangible actions and pursuits to bring them alive.

Explore new hobbies, community groups, events, classes, causes, adventures or learning experiences that make your heart sing. Let go of limiting stories about yourself that constrict possibilities.

Perhaps hidden interests wish to emerge now that emotional wounds no longer dominate your identity and choices. Release expectations and try something wildly creative or fun just for joy itself.

Ask yourself: "What would my daily activities look like if my primary goal was to inject as much significance as I could into my limited time on this planet?" Then, with determination, gradually take small strides toward your response.

Here are some additional prompts to spark ideas:

- What inspires sheer awe and wonder in you? Seek out those sensations.

- What did you love exploring as a child before fear or shame constricted you? Return to those innate passions.

- What bring you to flow states where time disappears? Immerse yourself there.

- What makes you feel fully alive and expressed? Unleash those energies creatively.

- How could you uplift and empower people who share your past struggles? Help others now that you know the way.

- What wisdom have you cultivated that the world desperately needs? Find avenues to share it.

In the words of Mahatma Gandhi, "Live as though tomorrow might be your last day, and learn as if you were going to live indefinitely." Inject every moment with enthusiasm and intent, maintaining an ongoing process of discovering meaning.

Continual Meaning Making

Rather than seeking a single epiphany for life purpose, remember meaning unfolds gradually through small acts of courage, creativity and compassion.

Each ordinary moment offers opportunity for meaning making. Even modest experiences like preparing food with care, having sincere conversations, being fully present on a walk, or brightening someone's day with a smile or kind word hold powerful purpose. The key is shifting from unconscious living to imbuing deliberate intentionality into your choices - prioritizing values-based actions over default routines.

Strive to make frequent course corrections asking "Does this activity align with my growth and values?" Strive to match your authentic self with how you invest your valuable life energy.

By infusing attention and care into your unique path, you consecrate even simple moments as sacred. Your life becomes your meaning.

Serving the World's Needs

While personal healing is sacred, meaning multiplies exponentially when we direct hearts and hands outward to positively impact other living beings.

You need not become a full-time activist or change agent. But consider how volunteering occasionally for causes aligned with your values exponentially amplifies purpose.

From animal rescue, to mentoring youth, to feeding the homeless, to ecological restoration, to visiting isolated elders, try on roles of service. Through contributing your gifts, you transcend past pain by making new waves of goodness.

Even small acts of kindness toward strangers like holding a door, cleaning up trash, giving food to someone in need or helping carry a heavy load reconnect us to our shared humanity. Just be the change you wish to see. The world will light up brighter.

Though wounds may linger, you possess the medicine. Share it.

Continual Rebirth

As you shed limiting past identities and consciously cultivate new purpose moving forward, consider enacting rituals to consecrate your growth and the ongoing process of identity expansion.

Rites of passage guide transitions by honoring the death of outgrown aspects and celebrating the emergence of new more mature parts of ourselves.

Try activities like:

- Creating rituals with music, poetry, imagery or items symbolically representing your changes
- Allowing yourself to grieve what is lost while embracing what is gained
- Sharing your growth journey with supportive loved ones
- Letting go of old belongings signifying your past self
- Enacting ceremonies to welcome your new chapter with intention
- Making space in your home environment to represent your present priorities
- Revisiting old journal entries to appreciate how far you've come
- Visualization meditations to crystallize new identities and strengths
- Creating art, poems, songs, or stories expressing your becoming

Rituals help mindfully honor and integrate each phase of our ongoing unfolding.

Conclusion: Write Your Story Anew

Tremendous joy awaits as you infuse life's raw materials with new meaning and purpose. How will you transmute past pain into future service?

Your expanded Self now integrates all experiences - dark and light - as teachers on the path of growth. While shadows come and go like passing clouds, your inner light remains unchanged.

Past pain is no longer protagonist but wise mentor. So take heart. Dance with life generously. The next beautiful chapter awaits your creation. Write it with courage.

Chapter 10: Continuing the Journey of Growth and Healing

What a profound journey you've courageously undertaken - facing emotional wounds from the past, cultivating mindfulness and self-compassion, processing painful memories, reframing stories, enacting rituals, and infusing life with new meaning after healing. You should feel immense pride in your commitment.

Yet as we've discussed, healing is a lifelong path rather than a single destination. While this marks the end of our formal time together, your own journey still stretches forward with much transformational terrain left to explore.

This final chapter offers guidance on how to keep growing beyond this book - to continually blossom into your highest potentials through ongoing self-care, embodiment practices, vulnerability, and meaning-making long after turning the final page.

I offer these parting thoughts not as prescriptive commandments, but as sparks to illuminate your way as you move ahead with courage into your own light. You are the sole author of your healing narrative. May you keep writing it with radical self-compassion.

Commit to Daily Inner Work

Remember that time alone does not heal emotional wounds without intention. Proactively dedicate time each day to some form of inner work based on your needs and personality: meditation, journaling, yoga, creative expression, mantras, therapy, etc.

Make self-care and growth practices non-negotiable priorities to integrate your emerging neural patterns and sustain emotional equilibrium. Even when busy, schedule activities nourishing your inner world, not just outer productivity.

Determine what ritual anchors your psyche each morning, and again helps you wind down peacefully each night. Bookend days with mindfulness. Keep cultivating mental spaciousness amidst life's inevitable chaos.

Keep Exploring Your Inner World

Regardless of how much you've grown already, remain ever-curious about your inner landscape through ongoing self-inquiry. Consider journaling reflection questions like:

- What feelings, memories, or patterns arise for me to observe and compassionately understand?

- How do I relate to myself and others differently now after doing this healing work?

- What core wounds or attachments still unconsciously influence my behaviors and reactions?
- How have my priorities and values shifted based on my growth?
- What new potentials or directions now feel aligned to explore?
- What insights arose today from being fully present?

Let self-examination become lifetime practice. Always seek deeper truth over comfort. Core convictions will continue evolving wildly. Moment to moment, meet your experience with mindfulness.

Release Judgments About Your Journey

Have patience and release attachment to linear healing. Personal growth is messy, unpredictable, and ever-changing. You may experience emotional setbacks, delays in intended changes, or new wounds. Meet it all with gentleness.

Rather than judging yourself when you slip into old reactive patterns, simply begin again. Progress flows in spirals, not straight lines. Just return to mindfulness and self-compassion. Your only "failure" is giving up.

Trust that by continually taking small steps forward, new life gradually emerges from ashes of the old. Even with the occasional setback, progress is still being made in an upward direction. Keep walking.

Don't Personalize Difficult Emotions

Remember that feelings come and go like passing weather. Don't assume every emotional storm reveals something flawed within you. You need not fix or get rid of periodic grief, anger, sadness or fear. Mindfully acknowledge difficult emotions with curiosity when they arise, allow them space to move through without judgment or storylines, then gently return to presence.

Getting comfortable "being with" all temporary inner states is the work. The right to exist belongs to all parts. Remain patiently present.

Retain Beginner's Mind

Resist the trap of complacency or premature closure on your healing journey. Question rigid stories you build even about your "reconstruction."

Approach experiences with fresh eyes unclouded by yesterday's insights. Find wonder hiding within mundane moments. See from love rather than learned limitations. Wisdom is released when we admit how little we know.

Empty your cup often. Whatever sense of "awakening" you experience is but a single frame in a film strip stretching to infinity. There is always more growth ahead.

Integrate Your Shadow

Feelings like resentment, anger, lust, greed, jealousy and pettiness are normal facets of being human. Yet we often reject these aspects as "unspiritual" which breeds inner division.

Integrate your full humanity by compassionately understanding rejected emotions when they inevitably arise within you rather than judging them as pathological. Make space for your wholeness.

In the words of the poet Rumi: "Embrace all that unfolds in your life, be it beautiful or frightening. Persevere through it all, for no emotion is everlasting." Cultivate a connection with every aspect of yourself, as suppressing your feelings is a form of harm.

Recognize Oneness in All

When you catch yourself judgmentally labeling others, remember we all exhibit "negative" behaviors in different contexts. We share the core conditions of wanting love, security and validation.

Convert harsh perceptions into understanding by considering others' unresolved hurts shaping their actions. Beneath behaviors lies shared humanity. We differ only in conditioning.

This empathetic perspective reduces resentment and facilitates forgiveness. Compassion reveals our unbreakable unity. Practice seeing all people as damaged healers, just like you.

Make Amends Courageously

Consider if past actions while unconsciously ruled by emotional wounds caused harm to others. Where appropriate, take courageous responsibility to apologize, make amends and change hurtful behaviors without expecting anything in return.

Cleaning your side of the street through non-egoic accountability and restitution where meaningful can powerfully heal pain between yourself and others. It also builds integrity to not evade hard reflections about ways you may have contributed to relationship challenges. Sincere atonement requires radical self-honesty.

Keep Sharing Your Gifts

Remember that one key to deriving meaning from hardship lies in humbly offering your unique gifts, perspectives and experiences to help guide others through similar struggles.

Your wounds bestow sacred duty to apply your healing toward alleviating suffering in the world. Let compassion flow selflessly through you. See your pain made purposeful through service. Discover just how much beauty you have to give.

Stay Rooted in Self-Care

On this never-ending journey of growth, regularly return to the same simple self-care practices that lovingly sustain body, mind and spirit:

Daily movement, hydration and nutrition

- Sufficient sleep and rest

- Meaningful social connection

- Silence, nature and mindfulness

- Taking time for unfettered joy and play

- Expressing your unique creative energies

Make self-care the solid bedrock supporting your continued
unfolding. Fortify your foundation, simplifying life to its essence.
Protect your peace fiercely yet gently.

Trust the Journey

When you inevitably encounter the unknown on the winding
path of healing: have courage.

New directions or callings may seem to lead you temporarily away
from cherished identities, beliefs, communities or dreams. But if
guided by intuition rather than fear, unexpected twists and turns
serve your expansion even when ego resists.

Surrender stories of how things "should be." Life's mysteries work
on scales far grander than our limited vision can perceive. Abide in
Source always for guidance. The universe delivers you exactly
where you need to go. Know this in your bones.

Remember sempre carpe diem - "always seize the day." Meet
each moment in wide-eyed wonder at the gift of being. Hold even
pain gently, allowing everything to transform you. The only real
failure is resisting experience.

Dance with the grace you find deep in darkness, becoming who you must. Growth requires surrendering learned limits for vaster belonging to eternal unfolding mystery. This is your eternal awakening.

And So We Begin...

More than an ending, this marks commencement of a new leg on the eternal journey we all share as spiritual beings having a temporary human experience. We walk this road together, even when paths diverge.

My deepest hope is that through this material, you have discovered renewed faith in your own intrinsic strength, worthiness, and potential to bring beauty from darkness. I have great faith in you. Now have faith in yourself.

Stay curious, compassionate and courageous. Keep turning inward for truth. The purpose of your consciousness blooms each moment you water it with presence. You are the miracle this world needs. Go share your light.

With divine love,

Monday Farouq

Conclusion: Turning Hurt into Hope

When we first began this journey together, you carried painful emotional wounds from the past that exerted quiet yet profound influence over your sense of identity, relationships, and possibilities in life. Like tangled barbed wire, old traumas, betrayals, losses, and patterns of abuse or neglect had ensnared your spirit in suffering, restricting your capacity to open fully into each precious moment with trust, intimacy, and purpose.

In response to childhood wounds, your mind and nervous system had adapted in ways that continued generating feelings of anxiety, shame, anger, numbness, perfectionism, and low self-worth. You related to yourself with relentless inner criticism, perpetuating childhood patterns of self-attack that decimated your self-confidence. Habitual negative thought loops like "I'm worthless," "I'm unlovable," "I'm defective," clouded your sight. Suffering felt inescapable.

Yet with great courage, you embarked on an intensive path of healing work to finally liberate yourself - and your future - from the shackles of past pain.

You learned first to identify, feel, and release suppressed emotions like grief, anger, fear, and shame that had ossified around old wounds. Through mindfulness practices, you cultivated equanimity to sit with discomfort and stay present. You strengthened the muscle of compassionate inner awareness.

By digging up traumatic memories and core beliefs formed in childhood, you traced the roots of present struggles back to formative experiences that had destined you to repeat cycles of hurt endlessly. Only through this radical self-inquiry could you finally rewrite constrictive internal narratives.

With care and insight, you learned to question ingrained assumptions, expand limiting perspectives, and shift from disempowering perceptions to empowering possibilities. The weight of old pain gradually lifted as you reframed the meaning of events from the wise vantage of your adult self.

You healed fractured pieces of yourself through practices of inner child work. By mourning unmet needs, reframing traumatic events, and re-parenting yourself with compassion, you integrated disowned parts of your being previously left abandoned in the past.

In safe community with others, you opened up about your darkness to no longer carry secret shame alone. This vulnerable sharing dissolved isolation. You learned that your story, while unique, was also universal. A sense of oneness emerged from realizing we all carry wounds alongside immense beauty. Connection healed.

Drawing meaning from past adversity, you reframed traumatic events not as curses dooming you, but as catalysts fatefully chosen for your highest growth. With gratitude, you embraced exactly where life had led, owning your struggles as stepping stones to strength, purpose, and compassion. Glimmers of wisdom arose revealing that the destination had been worth the journey.

By taking steps aligned with your authentic priorities and values, you began infusing each day with more meaning, adventure, love, and joy. You consciously filled life with passions that lit you up from the inside out. Through serving others, your suffering grew purposeful. Darkness transformed into destiny.

Of course, healing has no single final destination. It is a ceaseless journey without finite end. But the practices you engaged equipped you with a mindful resilience to skillfully stay present with all that arises on the eternal path - integrating pain when it cycles back, while steadily keeping your eyes uplifted towards the light.

While your wounded inner child still holds your hand, you now lead with the compassion and courage of your wise inner mentor to navigate challenges. You've begun awakening from the trance of past pain into direct experiential being. Equanimity guides rather than reactivity. This presence opens space for grace.

By bravely confronting the darkness, you discovered you were never separate from light in the first place. You simply came home to who you already were beneath it all - the boundlessly perfect essence that always awaited your return.

So, take heart. What had felt so broken inside can never be destroyed. It can only be forgotten temporarily, until we remember. Your luminous inner wholeness, unmarred by time and trials, patiently awaited this resurrection inside you all along.

You have now reclaimed the eternal wisdom which cannot be spoken, yet infuses these words. May you continue living it. The treasure was never hidden far away. It was here, reflected in stillness behind eyes that gazed back at you from the mirror. You needn't search any further.

Once lost, now found again. Welcome home.

On this day, you have fully given yourself permission to rest in your natural state of perfection just as you are - without barriers, beliefs or requirements. This unconditional self-acceptance alone heals.

The peace you sought tirelessly outside begins to well up inside, as the unified source of mind, body and spirit you knew as a child comes back online, having patiently awaited this homecoming.

Tend this inner flame gently yet fiercely. It is your connection to the eternal. With care, it illuminates each alive moment from within to guide your return to natural presence beyond learned limitations. This light transcends yet includes all form.

May we never forget the sacred future seeded inside this very moment. Here, now, is where you always awaken. The 1% change in trajectory shifts all. Infuse this breath, step and blink with holy purpose. Sacredness lives in the spaces between seconds when we return to the only home that was ever real - hidden inside your beating heart awaiting discovery, so you may uncover divinity right where you stand.

Remember this feeling of being emotionally and spiritually renewed by your courageous inner work. When inevitable challenges arise, recall that you've overcome far greater trials already. Stay humble yet bold in carrying onward.

We heal not to escape hardship, but to deepen ability to drink difficulty like clean water - being nourished rather than poisoned. This journey has prepared you. Now you must live the wisdom into being.

As your perception expands, may you behold the singular perfection of our shared human experience - that beneath surface chaos, everything is happening exactly as it must for our highest growth. We are all visitors navigating challenges that strengthen soul. Not one tear, breath or heartbeat is wasted.

There are no wrong paths, because your destiny was written across your every footstep before time itself. You cannot fail to become who you must be. Release outdated constraints of how you "should" feel. There is only this pure moment of fully feeling to liberate you.
Everything you need has always lived inside your empty hands, awaiting notice. You can rest now. This moment is complete; you are Home. Of this I am certain.

May these words stay close as you continue the next leg of this never ending journey of healing, awakening, and mystical homecoming. When lonely, lost or afraid, recall your eternal essence cannot be harmed—only temporarily forgotten until you claim it again today. This moment ever awaits your return.

You've been so very brave. Please care for yourself with the tenderness you now see you were always worthy of receiving. You've always been loved. And you always will be.

This is my promise.

Onward, with devotion...

About the Author

Monday Farouq is an author and psychologist passionate about helping people transform emotional wounds into wisdom. Leveraging his extensive training in trauma recovery, mindfulness practices, and personal growth work, he wrote "From Hurt to Healing" to guide readers through evidence-based strategies to process past pain, rewrite limiting beliefs, and step into greater freedom. Monday draws upon his own healing journey to empower individuals to break free from destructive patterns, integrate disowned parts of themselves with compassion, and live with meaning. He resides in Lagos, Nigeria where he serves as a rehabilitation consultant and volunteers to support addiction recovery in underserved communities. Monday continues sharing his message of resilience so that our deepest hurts may blossom into our greatest gifts.

www.ingramcontent.com/pod-product-compliance
Lightning Source LLC
Chambersburg PA
CBHW070910260726
48661CB00004B/1686